for Mandy
    J.H.P.

for Jim
    K.S.P.

Other books
by Kate Salley Palmer
published by Warbranch Press, Inc.

The Little Chairs (ISBN 0966711424)
The Pink House (ISBN 0966711416)
A Gracious Plenty (ISBN 0966711408)
Palmetto – Symbol of Courage (ISBN 0966711440)

*Almost Invisible: Black Patriots of the
American Revolution* (ISBN 0966711467)

www.warbranchpress.com

WARBRANCH PRESS, INC.

The illustrations were produced digitally on a Power Mac G4 Computer

Printed in the United States of America by Electric City Printing in Anderson, South
Carolina

ISBN 0966711459

Published by Warbranch Press, Inc.
329 Warbranch Rd.
Central, SC 29630

Third Printing

FRANCIS MARION AND THE LEGEND OF

The SwampFox

by Kate Salley Palmer

Illustrated by James H. Palmer, Jr.

"Our band is few, but true and tried,
Our leader, frank and bold;
The British Soldier trembles
When Marion's name is told."

A poet named William Cullen Bryant wrote those lines. He was describing a legendary South Carolina military leader named Francis Marion and the soldiers who followed him. They fought during the American Revolution, a war that occurred more than two hundred years ago when the thirteen American colonies were fighting to be free from British rule.

Between 1780 and 1782, three important American patriot leaders emerged in South Carolina.

Andrew Pickens

One was Andrew Pickens, whose men fought in the northwestern section of South Carolina.

Thomas Sumter

Another was Thomas Sumter, who led an army in the middle of the state. Sumter was a bold commander who liked to wear a gamecock feather in his cap. This earned him the nickname, the "Gamecock."

Francis Marion

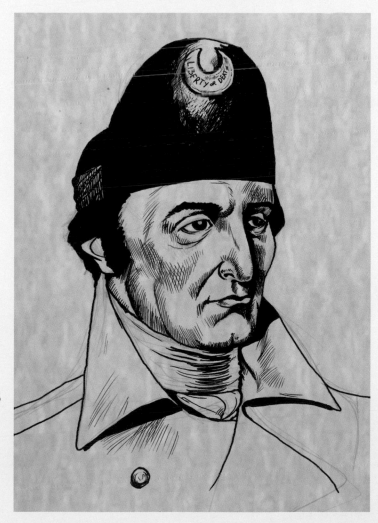

The most famous of the three, Francis Marion, commanded a force of mostly volunteer citizens, called militia, who fought in the eastern part of the state. Marion was known for his surprise attacks near rivers like the Santee and Peedee- attacks which made it difficult for the British and their local supporters, called Tories, to move men and supplies.

Francis Marion never got caught. After a battle, he and his men would disappear into the swamps and forests they knew so well.

Oddly, it was a British officer who gave Marion his nickname.

This brutal officer, Colonel Banastre Tarleton, commanded a famous fighting force known as the "Green Dragoons" because the soldiers rode horseback and wore green coats.

Once, after a battle, Francis Marion and his band of ragged volunteers led an angry Tarleton and his dragoons on a furious twenty-six mile, seven-hour chase through swampland full of insects, snakes and alligators. When they reached a place called "Ox Swamp," Tarleton stopped.

His men were tired and hungry. Even the horses were breathing heavily. There was no sign of Marion or his men.

Slowly, Colonel Tarleton turned his horse around. "Come, boys! Let's go back and we will catch the Gamecock," he said, "But as for this...old fox, the Devil himself could not catch him!"

Everyone began to call Francis Marion the "Swamp Fox."

The "Swamp Fox" was born in 1732 at Goatfield Plantation in St. John's Parish, Berkeley, South Carolina. Now the area is called Berkeley County. In Colonial times, South Carolina was divided into districts and parishes, not counties.

Francis was the youngest of six children born to Gabriel and Esther Marion, who were French Huguenots. Their families had left France to avoid religious persecution. The Marion family, like most of their neighbors, farmed their land. Francis was a small and sickly child, but he enjoyed exploring the swampland for many miles around his home--camping, fishing, and hunting.

Francis Marion was especially close to his older brothers, Job and Gabriel. As an adult, he often felt at home at Belle Isle, Gabriel's farm on the Santee River. Farms and plantations, much like the ones the Marions worked, produced such crops as rice and indigo.

South Carolina was one of the richest colonies in America, because the planters had many African slaves to help them grow large quantities of crops the British needed. Rice and indigo, along with many other products, were sent to England by ships out of Charleston harbor.

As a young man, Francis Marion volunteered to help fight the Cherokee in the Blue Ridge region in the foothills and in the mountains near the border of South Carolina and North Carolina.

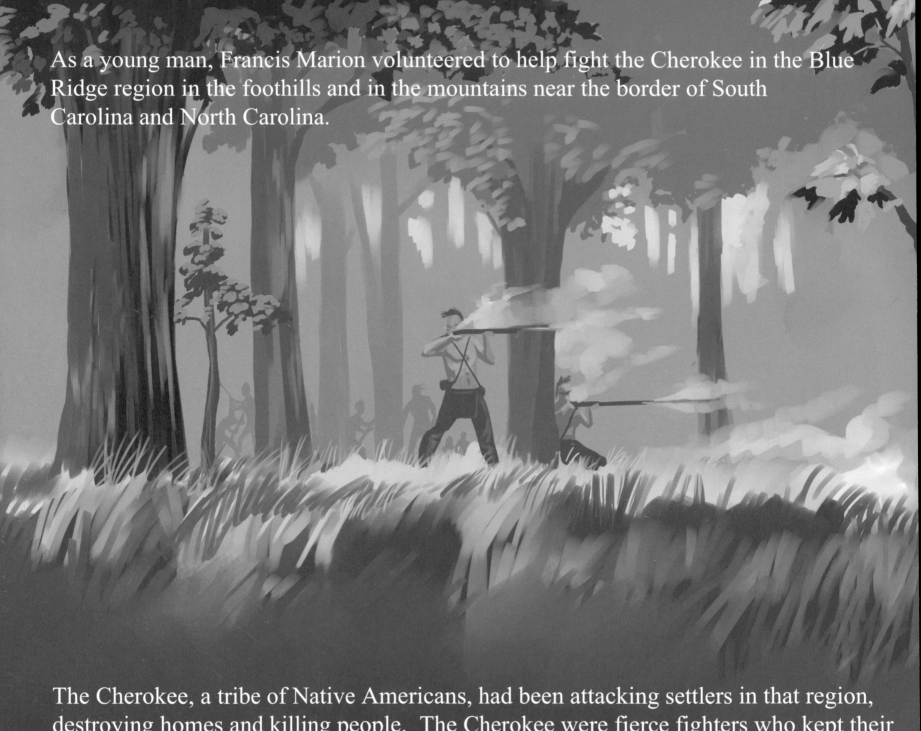

The Cherokee, a tribe of Native Americans, had been attacking settlers in that region, destroying homes and killing people. The Cherokee were fierce fighters who kept their enemies off guard with rapid surprise, ambush and retreat. After a battle, they were able to disappear into the forests of their territory.

Marion fought bravely. At one point, he personally led soldiers through a dangerous battle to victory. Later, as a militia leader in the Revolutionary War, he would successfully use the Cherokee tactics of stealth, ambush, retreat and surprise against the British.

Francis Marion went back to farming when the Cherokee War was over. He was a serious, hardworking man who did not brag or even talk about his impressive experience in backcountry warfare.

His reputation for bravery and modesty earned him the respect of his neighbors, and they elected him to the First South Carolina Provincial Congress, which met in Charleston in 1775.

When the American Revolutionary War began at Lexington, Massachusetts, South Carolina's Provincial Congress met and formed three military regiments. Francis Marion was elected captain in the Second South Carolina Regiment. Colonel William Moultrie, the regiment's leader, designed their uniforms. They wore blue coats trimmed in red and black caps with a silver crescent on the front.

The Second Regiment 's flag was blue with a white crescent in the corner. The flag may have had the word "Liberty" in white across the bottom.

One of the most famous battles fought by the Second Regiment was on Sullivan's Island, across the harbor from Charleston. There, Colonel Moultrie and the Second Regiment built a fort of palmetto logs and beach sand to repel a fleet of British ships, which tried to sail into Charleston harbor and capture the city of Charleston.

The soldiers of the Second Regiment were saved in that battle by their bravery and by the fort they had built. Cannonballs from the ships sank harmlessly into the soft logs and sand, without knocking down the walls of the fort. South Carolinians were so grateful for the victory that they proclaimed the palmetto tree to be the state tree, and placed a picture of it on the blue flag.

Francis Marion, by then a major, commanded some of the fort's guns at Sullivan's Island on that day, June 28, 1776. His men aimed carefully at the ships, helping to inflict so much damage that the British were forced to sail away, defeated.

The log fort on Sullivan's Island was named "Fort Moultrie," for the commander of the Second Regiment.

The city of Charleston later fell to a larger British force in 1780. By that time, Colonel Moultrie had been promoted to general. Francis Marion then became "Lt. Colonel Francis Marion, Commandant of the Second Regiment."

Before Charleston was captured, General Moultrie ordered all officers who were ill or unfit for duty to leave the city at once.

Marion had just broken his ankle. That may not seem like a lucky thing, but in 1780, it was lucky for Marion, for South Carolina, and for the American colonies. His leg still swollen and useless, Marion had to be carried out of Charleston on a litter. His friend, Col. Peter Horry, also left the city because of his severe rheumatism.

When the British arrived in Charleston, all the remaining regimental officers were taken prisoner.
Francis Marion went home to the Santee River and disappeared among his friends and family. He remained free to continue the fight against the British.
Lord Cornwallis, commander of the British forces in America, took command in Charleston, and planned his attacks from there.

Once the British had taken Charleston, they thought that the rest of South Carolina would fall easily, giving them clear passage to the north, where they expected to defeat General George Washington's Continental Army.

Major General Horatio Gates, commander of the Continental Army in the South, ordered all southern officers who were still free to ride north and meet his Continental Army near Camden, South Carolina.

Francis Marion, Peter Horry, and others put their uniforms back on in spite of their injuries, and rode boldly northward to meet General Gates.

When they arrived at the Continental Army's camp, Marion and his small band of men, many of whom were farmers in homespun clothing, did not make a favorable impression.

A Continental Army officer described them: "Col. Marion, a gentleman of South Carolina [had] very few followers, only about twenty men and boys, some white, some black...all on horseback, most of them miserably equipped; [they wore] small leather caps [and] wretched clothing."

Their appearance was so comical, wrote the officer, that other officers of the Continental Army had a hard time keeping the regular soldiers from laughing at them.

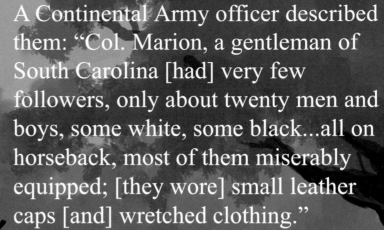

General Gates wanted to get rid of Marion, sending him to the interior of South Carolina with orders to spy on the enemy and make reports.

This was just what Francis Marion wanted. He knew that some South Carolina militia leaders, such as Major John James, had formed groups of citizen volunteers to fight the British and Tories.

Marion believed that militia groups like this would play an important role in defending the American colonies.

James had asked for a commander. With permission from Gates, Marion rode away immediately to take command of the Williamsburg militia.

Marion's brigade reached the Williamsburg militia encampment late the next afternoon, where they received a quite different welcome than the one the Continental Army had given them. Here, Marion heard shouts and other exclamations of joy. Many of the men recognized their new commander, having served under him or having seen him while serving in other militia groups.

Major James dashed up to welcome Marion and his men. He introduced the new commander to his officers and men. Then, Major James called up his fifteen-year-old son, William.

Many years later, writing about Francis Marion, that boy, William James, described his first sight of the man who would become known as the "Swamp Fox."

"He was below the middle stature of men," wrote James,

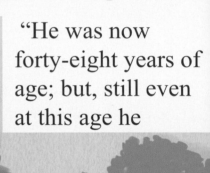

"His body was well set, but his knees and ankles were badly formed; and he still limped upon one leg.

[The expression on his face] was remarkably [calm]; his forehead was large and high, and his eyes black and piercing."

His nose was large and hooked, his chin protruded.

"He was now forty-eight years of age; but, still even at this age he was capable of enduring fatigue and every [hardship] necessary to a partisan. He was dressed in a close round-bodied crimson jacket, of a coarse texture, and he wore a leather cap, part of the uniform of the Second Regiment, with a silver crescent in front, inscribed with the words, 'Liberty or Death.'"

The only record we have of Marion's appearance are his soldiers' written descriptions of him.

There were no cameras back then, and Marion never sat for a portrait.

Upon taking command of Major James' force, Marion wasted no time. He led his men right away on boat-burning excursions up and down the Santee River. They burned or destroyed every transport the British might use to cross the waterways. As they carried out their mission, news reached them of General Gates's defeat at Camden.

The American Continental Army had suffered great losses at Camden. Many soldiers were killed and captured. Almost all of the American cannons, ammunition and supplies were captured, and between 900 and 1,000 American soldiers were taken prisoner.

General Gates had fled to Charlotte on horseback, leaving the defeated army behind.

More bad news for the Americans came with reports that Thomas Sumter's army, unaware of the defeat at Camden, had been overtaken by Tarleton and attacked at a place called Fishing Creek, near the Catawba River. The British took weapons, supplies, and more than 300 prisoners of war.

Marion's militia was now the only fighting force left in South Carolina to battle the British and Tory soldiers.

From their well-hidden camps in the Peedee swamps, Marion's brigade ventured out to make life miserable for their enemies, attacking their positions, and stealing their supplies. Marion's men slept in swamp shadows during the day and moved to attack at night. Marion had a network of scouts and spies reporting to him on the movements of the enemy. But he rarely told anyone of his own plan of action. He kept his intentions secret until the last moment, when he finally told his men what to do.

Eluding British patrols, Francis Marion took his men south to watch the main road from Camden to Charleston. Through his spies, he learned that a small British force was guarding prisoners and supplies at Nelson's Ferry, a place where they would cross the Santee River.

Marion attacked at first light with his small band of men, surprising the enemy before they could gather their weapons. Marion's men captured or killed a number of British and Tory troops, taking horses, weapons, and supplies.

But the big prize was 150 Continental soldiers from Maryland whom the British had captured at Camden less than a week before. Trained soldiers were in short supply, so Marion freed them to continue their fight against the British.

Most of the freed Continentals refused to go with Marion's group and many others deserted. Perhaps they were among those who had laughed at the appearance of Marion's men before the battle of Camden.

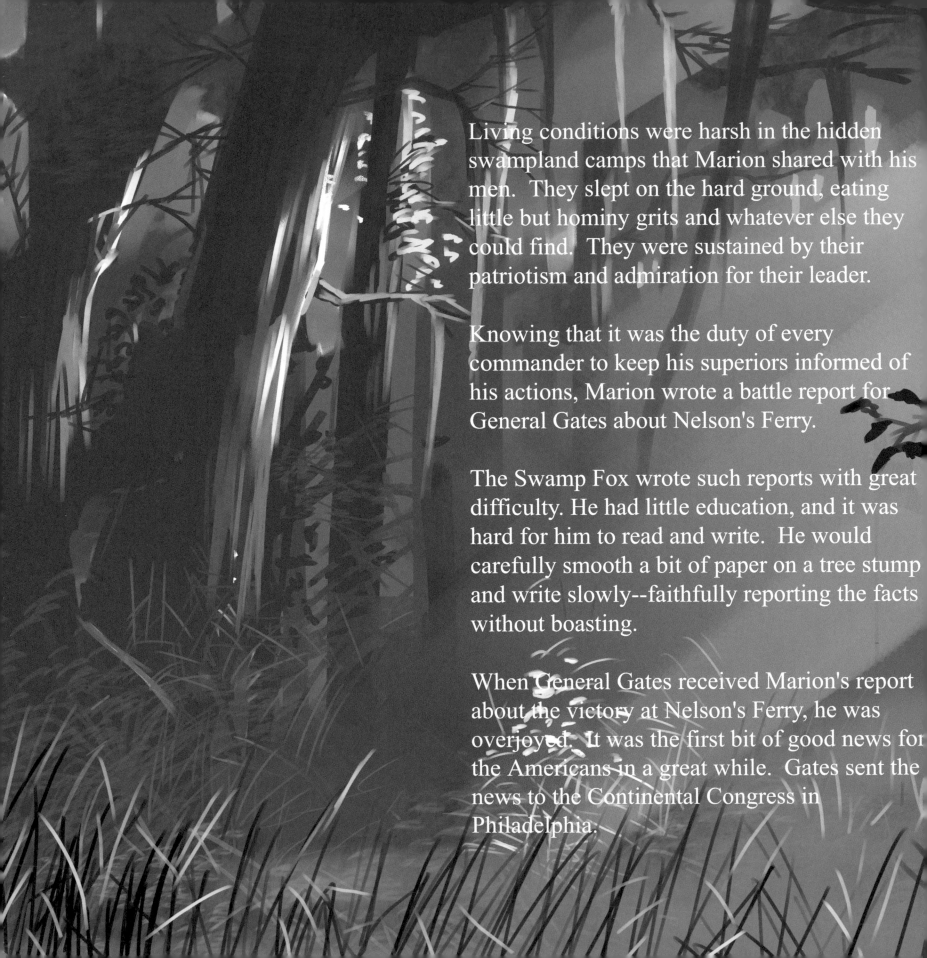

Living conditions were harsh in the hidden swampland camps that Marion shared with his men. They slept on the hard ground, eating little but hominy grits and whatever else they could find. They were sustained by their patriotism and admiration for their leader.

Knowing that it was the duty of every commander to keep his superiors informed of his actions, Marion wrote a battle report for General Gates about Nelson's Ferry.

The Swamp Fox wrote such reports with great difficulty. He had little education, and it was hard for him to read and write. He would carefully smooth a bit of paper on a tree stump and write slowly--faithfully reporting the facts without boasting.

When General Gates received Marion's report about the victory at Nelson's Ferry, he was overjoyed. It was the first bit of good news for the Americans in a great while. Gates sent the news to the Continental Congress in Philadelphia.

The Congress reported to newspapers all over the colonies. This made "Francis Marion" a well-known name throughout the country.

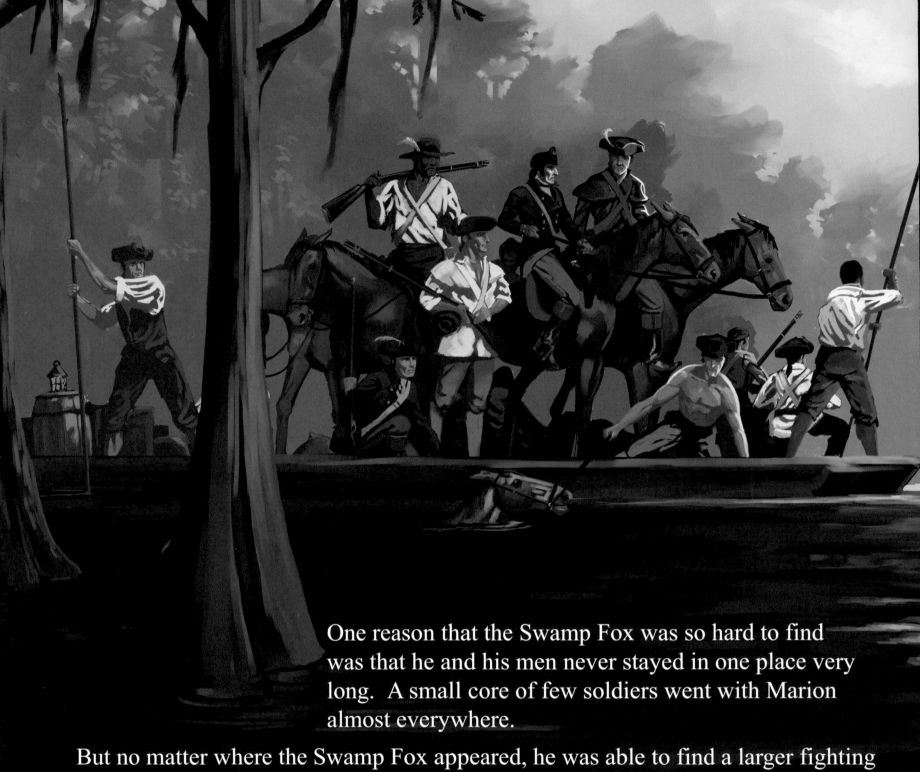

One reason that the Swamp Fox was so hard to find
was that he and his men never stayed in one place very
long. A small core of few soldiers went with Marion
almost everywhere.

But no matter where the Swamp Fox appeared, he was able to find a larger fighting
force of volunteer militia ready to join him.
Often, after a battle, Marion's brigade would shrink again to only a few men.

The volunteer fighters were ordinary farmers who worried about their families, crops,
land and livestock. Marion, a compassionate leader, understood their concerns. He
knew that such volunteers did not have to follow military orders.

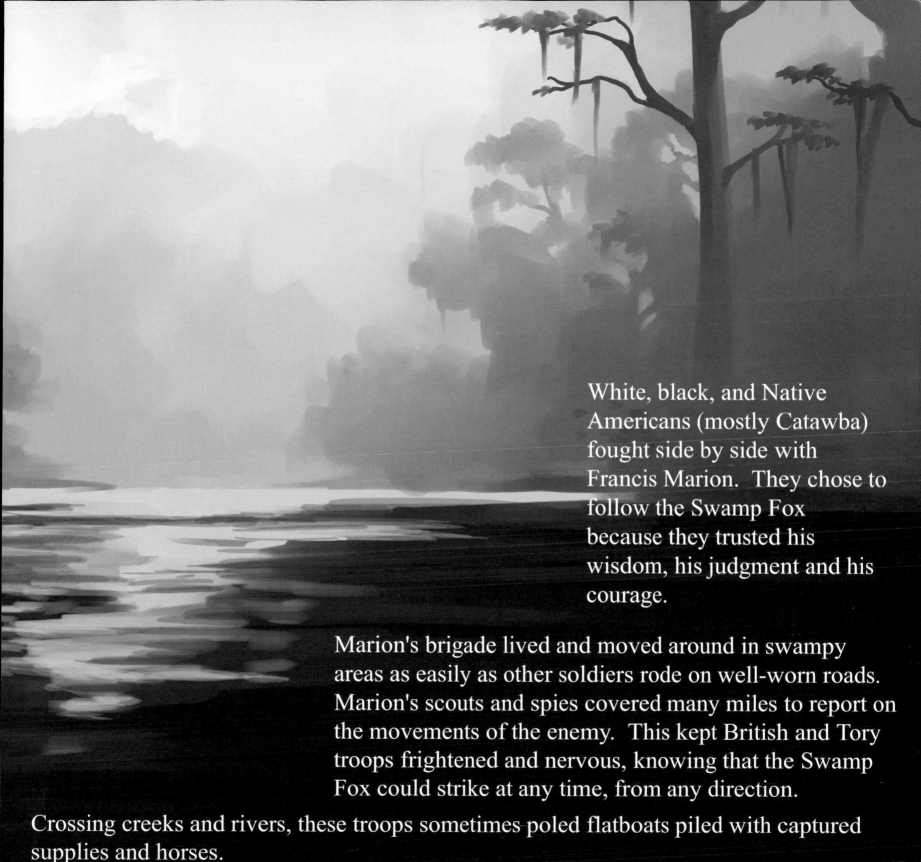

White, black, and Native Americans (mostly Catawba) fought side by side with Francis Marion. They chose to follow the Swamp Fox because they trusted his wisdom, his judgment and his courage.

Marion's brigade lived and moved around in swampy areas as easily as other soldiers rode on well-worn roads. Marion's scouts and spies covered many miles to report on the movements of the enemy. This kept British and Tory troops frightened and nervous, knowing that the Swamp Fox could strike at any time, from any direction.

Crossing creeks and rivers, these troops sometimes poled flatboats piled with captured supplies and horses.
Francis Marion could not swim, so he sometimes crossed waterways by clinging to his horse's saddle, letting the horse swim him across.

Lord Cornwallis became discouraged at the successes of American patriot leaders like Francis Marion. South Carolina was home to both American patriots and Tory loyalists, who had known one another as friends and neighbors, living peacefully before the war.
South Carolina communities containing both patriots and loyalists were torn apart by the struggle for American independence.

Even within some families, there were supporters of each side. A violent civil war erupted in the state after the fall of Charleston, fueled by the brutality of British officers like Tarleton, James Wemyss, and others. Through their cruel behavior toward all the citizens of South Carolina, the British became their own worst enemies. They raged about, hanging farmers, burning crops and homes, killing livestock, and threatening women and children.

Individuals changed sides often-and eventually began to favor the patriot cause, due to the cruelty of the British.

Though other patriots and their leaders behaved as cruelly to Tories as the British had behaved toward them, Francis Marion did not. Marion was a compassionate man, and knew that after the fighting was over, the former enemies would have to live together in peace again. On many occasions, he saved Tories from death after patriots had captured them.

Marion continued his harassment of the enemy. Receiving information that a group of Tory soldiers under the command of Colonel John Ball was camped at Shepherd's Ferry, near the Black River at a place called "Black Mingo Swamp,"
The Swamp Fox decided to drive the Tories out of that area. Again, Marion attacked at night.

The Tories heard the hoofbeats of Marion's horses on a bridge and were able to prepare themselves. Marion's force attacked on three sides, and many of the Tories fled into the woods. Colonel Ball was killed. Marion captured his fine thoroughbred horse, renamed him "Ball," and rode him for the rest of the war.

A month after Black Mingo, Marion learned of a Tory force camped at Tearcoat Swamp, about twenty-five miles north of Nelson's Ferry. By this time, the Swamp Fox commanded about 150 men-his largest force yet. Again, Marion's men struck from three sides under cover of darkness. This time, Marion lost no men, and was able to capture horses and supplies enough to equip even more volunteers.

With the defeat at Tearcoat Swamp, Tory support for the British in the Santee-Peedee area of South Carolina shrank.

Marion's ability to strike at will against British and Tory posts and then melt back into the forests meant that the British couldn't safely contact or supply their soldiers in the Peedee

But the British still held Charleston, which at that time was the capital of South Carolina. With his large, well-trained army, Lord Cornwallis felt he could overrun the state of South Carolina and move north to Virginia to attack George Washington's army.

Then, on October 5, 1780, in a move that would help Americans win the Revolution, the Continental Congress in Philadelphia finally allowed George Washington, the Commander-in-Chief of the American Continental Army, to replace General Horatio Gates with the man he had wanted all along to command the forces in the South.

General George Washington

Col. Henry "Light Horse Harry" Lee

That man, Major General Nathanael Greene of Rhode Island, was regarded as the most talented American commander next to Washington himself.

General Greene reached Charlotte, North Carolina, in early December and relieved General Horatio Gates of his command. There he found his Army in North Carolina to be small--less than 2,000 men--and poorly trained. They needed everything--weapons, food, equipment and training.

Though he knew of the patriot groups in South Carolina, Greene feared they would not be enough to stop Cornwallis's well-supplied, highly disciplined army of Regular, or professional, soldiers.

Greene and Washington hoped to build an army of American Regular soldiers, but that had not happened yet.

General Greene needed time.

General Nathanael Greene

He wanted Cornwallis's forces to stay so busy chasing "Gamecocks" and "Swamp Foxes" that he wouldn't be able to bring British soldiers into North Carolina and destroy Greene's army before the army was ready for battle.

With Greene came Col. Henry "Light Horse Harry" Lee, who would give valuable help to the Swamp Fox.

On New Year's Day, 1781, Francis Marion received a letter from South Carolina's Provincial Governor John Rutledge, who was in Philadelphia with the Continental Congress. The letter informed Marion that Governor Rutledge had appointed him to the rank of Brigadier General.

Rutledge had promoted the Swamp Fox because of his talent as a soldier and as a commander of men. Marion was stern with his men, knowing that military discipline could save their lives in battle. But he was also kind and sympathetic.

When his men had no blankets, General Marion slept on the cold ground without a blanket as well.

At about the same time, two British officers were chasing the Swamp Fox. They planned a trap for Marion to pin him down and prevent his escape.

John Watson led a force along the Peedee River and Welbore Doyle moved along Lynches River. They planned to meet where the two rivers came together. They didn't know exactly where Marion's camp was, but they were determined to find it.

Francis Marion knew that Watson and Doyle were looking for him. His scouts and spies tracked both groups.

Marion attacked Watson's army for several weeks. He attacked at every bridge and crossing point on the river, slowing the enemy and giving his men a chance to escape, for the two British officers were close.

Watson at last gave up and rode away, but Doyle went on to find the hideout, at a place called Snow's Island, where the Lynches and Peedee Rivers come together. Doyle attacked, killing or wounding several men left behind to guard it. But there were few supplies left to destroy, and most of Marion's men had already scattered.

General Nathanael Greene moved his small army into South Carolina, into the Cheraw area on the Peedee River.   There, he divided that force. The smaller of the two groups, under the command of Brigadier General Daniel Morgan, he sent toward western South Carolina. He sent the larger force, commanded by Lieutenant Colonel Henry "Light Horse Harry" Lee of Virginia, to support the Swamp Fox.
Lord Cornwallis had to abandon his planned march northward.

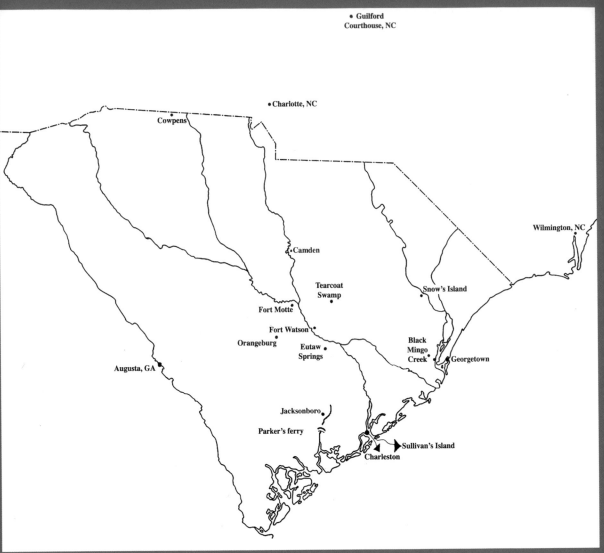

South and North Carolina Revolutionary War sites

He was forced to divide his own army to deal with the Americans now in South Carolina. He sent Colonel Tarleton after Daniel Morgan's army. Morgan's army and Tarleton's met and fought a battle at Cowpens, South Carolina.
The British army was overwhelmed at Cowpens.
Many of them were killed or taken prisoner. The Americans captured weapons and supply wagons.

Lord Cornwallis

News of the American victory at Cowpens thrilled the patriots, and Loyalists began to lose hope.

Cornwallis was trying to attack General Greene's army, but the Swamp Fox kept picking at him. Light Horse Harry Lee's army was chasing him too. He finally abandoned British outposts in South Carolina for his march north to fight Greene. British soldiers left behind had to deal with American partisan commanders such as Morgan, Pickens, and Marion.

By the time Cornwallis's army met Greene's army at Guilford Courthouse in North Carolina, both armies were exhausted and many were sick. It was a hard fight. Many many men were killed. The British were able to make the Americans leave the area, so they claimed victory. But there really was no winner. The British lost so many men and supplies that they were a defeated army after Guilford Court House.

The British army pushed weakly north to Virginia, but they had not been able to defeat South Carolina.

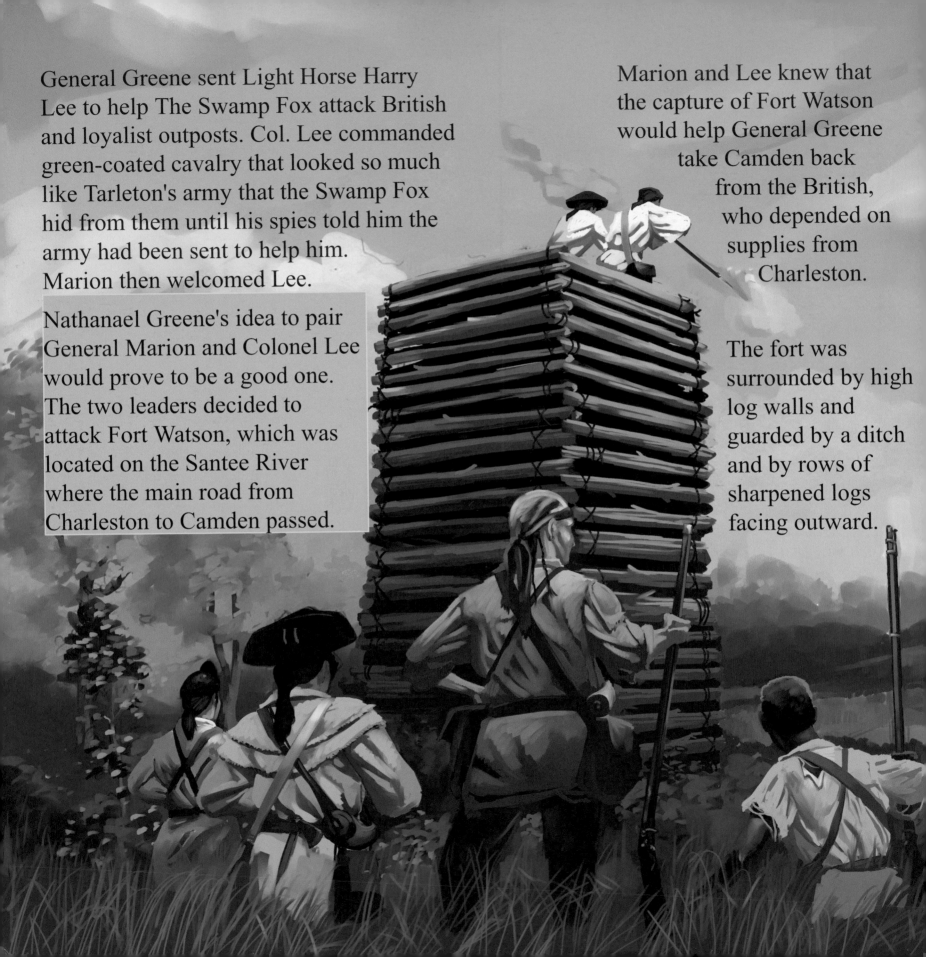

General Greene sent Light Horse Harry Lee to help The Swamp Fox attack British and loyalist outposts. Col. Lee commanded green-coated cavalry that looked so much like Tarleton's army that the Swamp Fox hid from them until his spies told him the army had been sent to help him. Marion then welcomed Lee.

Nathanael Greene's idea to pair General Marion and Colonel Lee would prove to be a good one. The two leaders decided to attack Fort Watson, which was located on the Santee River where the main road from Charleston to Camden passed.

Marion and Lee knew that the capture of Fort Watson would help General Greene take Camden back from the British, who depended on supplies from Charleston.

The fort was surrounded by high log walls and guarded by a ditch and by rows of sharpened logs facing outward.

British and loyalist troops held the fort.
Lee and Marion's men could not sneak up on it or
climb the walls. Then a militia officer named
Hezekiah Maham had an idea. During the night,
the patriots built a tower of logs. Sharpshooters
could stand tall behind log walls, high enough to
fire into the open space of the fort.

The soldiers inside Fort Watson were stunned when they
realized what was happening. Because of the
sharpshooters in the Maham Tower, they couldn't get
into the open for their weapons or gunpowder.
They couldn't fire their cannons, or even
reach food and water.

The British and Loyalists
surrendered to the Americans and
abandoned the fort.

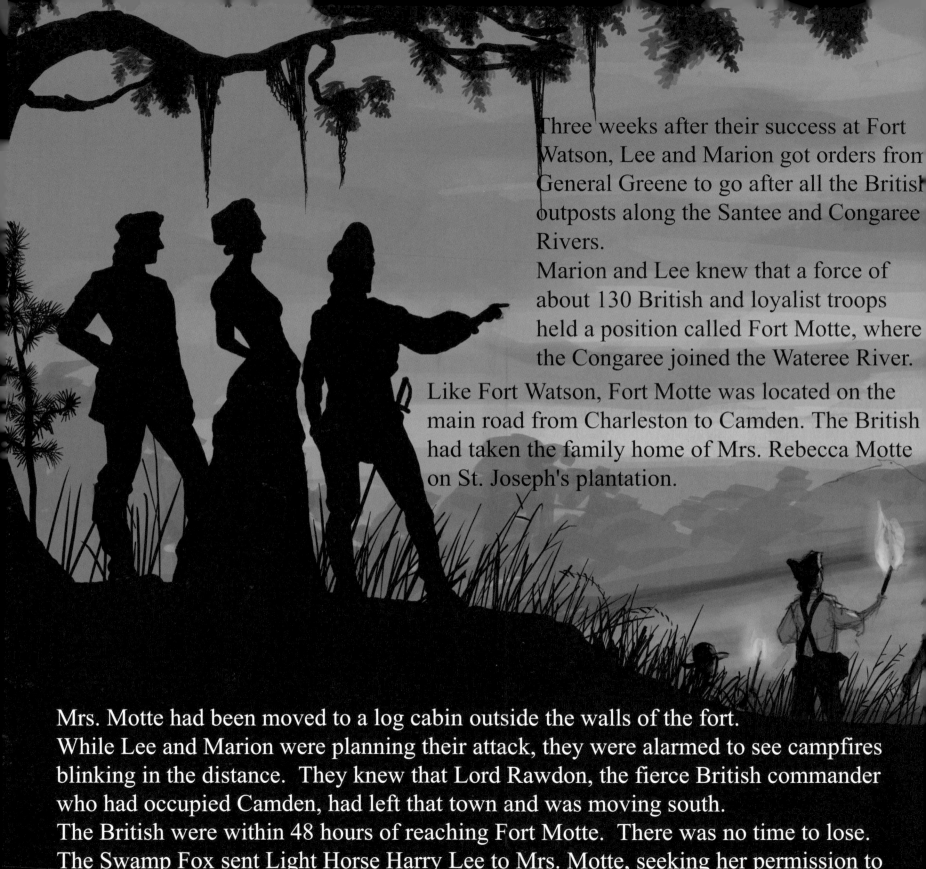

Three weeks after their success at Fort Watson, Lee and Marion got orders from General Greene to go after all the British outposts along the Santee and Congaree Rivers.

Marion and Lee knew that a force of about 130 British and loyalist troops held a position called Fort Motte, where the Congaree joined the Wateree River.

Like Fort Watson, Fort Motte was located on the main road from Charleston to Camden. The British had taken the family home of Mrs. Rebecca Motte on St. Joseph's plantation.

Mrs. Motte had been moved to a log cabin outside the walls of the fort.

While Lee and Marion were planning their attack, they were alarmed to see campfires blinking in the distance. They knew that Lord Rawdon, the fierce British commander who had occupied Camden, had left that town and was moving south.

The British were within 48 hours of reaching Fort Motte. There was no time to lose. The Swamp Fox sent Light Horse Harry Lee to Mrs. Motte, seeking her permission to burn her home by setting fire to the roof. Mrs. Motte enthusiastically agreed.

Some historians say she even offered a set of ceremonial fire arrows with which to start the fire. The Americans used fire arrows, but many fashioned fiery balls of tar and sulfur, flinging them to the roof with lengths of cloth, like slingshots.

The British surrendered right away, and Marion sent men to put out the fire. British and loyalists also helped douse the flames, and Mrs. Motte had a meal prepared for the American and British officers. As they were enjoying themselves, Marion heard that some of the American Continentals were abusing loyalists. Furious, he ran down to where American Continentals were trying to hang a South Carolinian who had been loyal to the British.

The Swamp Fox hated cruelty. He drew his sword.

"Cut him down! Cut him down!" He demanded. It was the only time on record that Marion ever drew his sword except in combat.

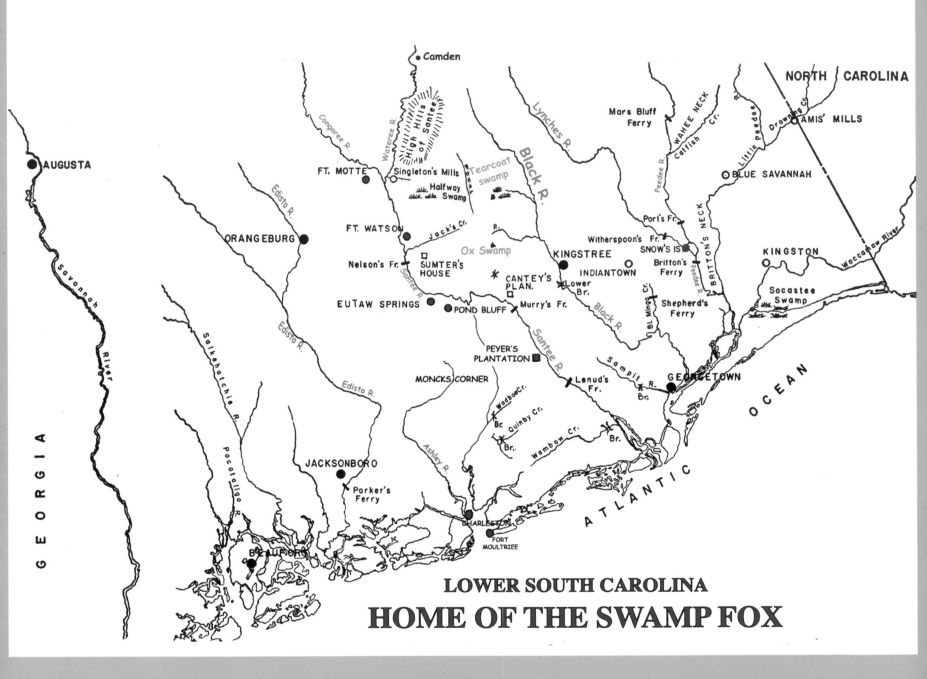

LOWER SOUTH CAROLINA

HOME OF THE SWAMP FOX

General Greene returned to South Carolina, sending American Continental soldiers to occupy Camden. They discovered that Lord Rawdon had destroyed the town before he left.

With General Greene's return to South Carolina, Marion's brigade became part of the American Continental Army. At his camp, Greene met with Lee and Marion for the first time. Greene and The Swamp Fox talked for hours, and came to admire one another tremendously. Greene laid out his plan to take back South Carolina.

THE MEN WHO MARCHED WITH MARION

Marion called his militia together and rode off down the Santee. He followed Rawdon south into St. Stephen's Parish, among his old friends and neighbors, where he had hunted and fished as a child. There, on Peyre's Plantation, he found another island hiding place for his camp. His men constructed shelters and gathered supplies.

Greene took his men and camped at a place called the High Hills of Santee, between the Santee and Lynches Rivers.
Marion continued to attack British and loyalist forces, retreating only when his brigade ran out of gunpowder.

General Greene wrote to Marion, "The gallantry and good conduct of your men reflects the highest honor on your brigade."

Soon, Light Horse Harry Lee's Cavalry, a group of Continental solders, and a force of South Carolinians commanded by General Greene began a march toward Charleston to take back the capital of South Carolina.

Greenc's South Carolina riflemen found their passage blocked by a British force which occupied a fortified plantation house in Eutaw Springs.

General Marion and his men rode to the aid of General Greene.

Eutaw Springs was a "pitched battle," meaning that rows of riflemen from each side met face to face and shot at one another on the field. Marion divided his riflemen, sending Daniel Morgan's men to one side and his to the other. Together, they advanced, shooting at the enemy. When they ran out of gunpowder, they had to withdraw. But Marion was proud of his men. They had fought with coolness and bravery under fire. They had done everything asked of them.

General Greene's army then marched south and surrounded Charleston. British troops there were preparing to leave.

Light Horse Harry Lee returned from Yorktown, Virginia, to report that Lord Cornwallis had surrendered his army to General Washington. Everyone knew that the war was all but over.

Governor Rutledge decided it was time to reestablish a government in South Carolina, and asked his military leaders to supervise an election. Several war heroes were elected to the State Senate, including Francis Marion.

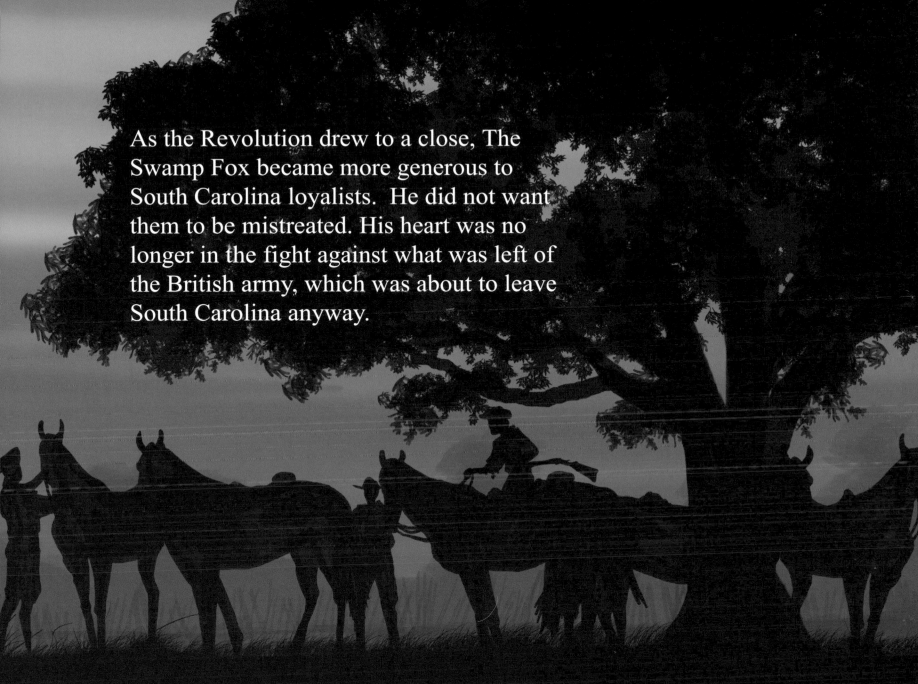

As the Revolution drew to a close, The Swamp Fox became more generous to South Carolina loyalists. He did not want them to be mistreated. His heart was no longer in the fight against what was left of the British army, which was about to leave South Carolina anyway.

On December 14, 1782, the British finally left Charleston. South Carolina militia groups all over the state disbanded. Hungry, ragged and unpaid, the heroes of the Revolution set out for their homes. General Marion dismissed his men with praise for their gallantry and courage, and his best wishes for their prosperity. Then he got on his horse, Ball, and headed for Pond Bluff. He found the home he had built in ruins. Armies of both sides had stolen his supplies and furniture. His house had been burned. He was now poor, but he bought feed, seed, and tools on credit so he could rebuild his life.

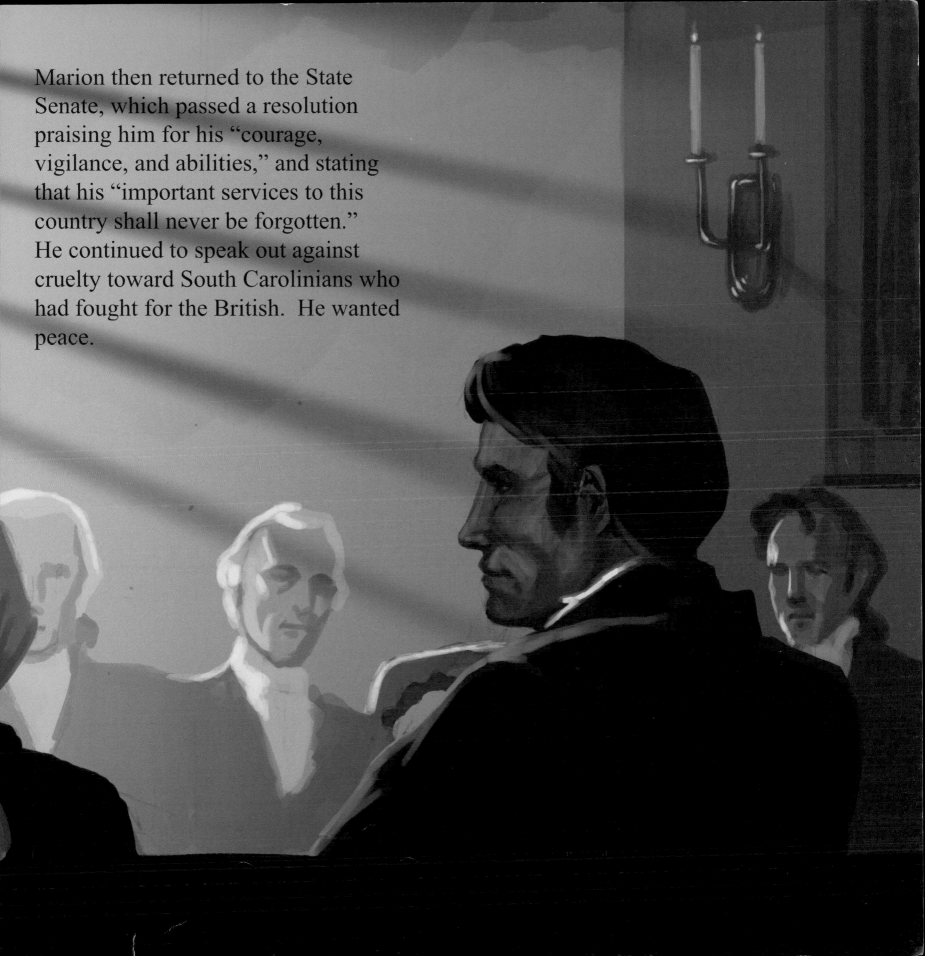

Marion then returned to the State Senate, which passed a resolution praising him for his "courage, vigilance, and abilities," and stating that his "important services to this country shall never be forgotten." He continued to speak out against cruelty toward South Carolinians who had fought for the British. He wanted peace.

Marion retired to his farm at Pond Bluff on the Santee River. He built a simple, one-story, unpainted home there, and farmed the land. Marrying late in life, he and his wife enjoyed riding horses and camping together in some of the places he had camped as a soldier. They never had any children.

The Swamp Fox died at Pond Bluff when he was sixty-three years old. On his deathbed, he told his wife that he was not sad or afraid to die, for he had never intentionally done harm to anyone. He was buried at Belle Isle, his brother Gabriel's home, where his tomb still stands next to that of his wife.

Pond Bluff today lies under the waters of Lake Marion, which provides hydroelectric power to the people who live now where the Marion family and their friends lived so many years ago. Several battle sites still exist in places where the Swamp Fox fought for South Carolina and the United States of America.

Thousands of South Carolinians named their children "Francis Marion." The hero became a legend.

GLOSSARY

Backcountry - Area of South Carolina from about 50 miles from the coast to the mountains.

Belle Isle - The plantation home of Gabriel Marion, Francis Marion's brother.

Brigade - A group of soldiers - for example, the men who followed Francis Marion.

Cavalry - Soldiers who went into battle on horses.

Colony - Before the Revolution, there were thirteen American colonies loyal to the King of England. After the Revolution these were states (The United States of America).

Continentals - The Regular Army made up from Americans from all the colonies.

Dragoons - Groups of mounted soldiers.

Green Dragoon - Mounted soldiers (cavalry) of Col. Banastre Tarleton - mostly made up of loyalist troops from New York and New Jersey.

Goatfield Plantation - Francis Marion's plantation in St. John's Parish

Guerrilla warfare - Hit and run warfare that relies on ambush, surprise, stealth for the raids and then forces melt back into the population before the enemy can react.

Huguenots - People who came to America because of religious persecution in France.

Homespun clothing - Clothes made from items grown on the farm, e.g., cotton, wool and animal skins.

Indigo - An important South Carolina crop before and during the Revolution. Parts of the indigo plant were used to make indigo blue dye. Many clothes worn by people of that time were the color indigo blue. The South Carolina flag and the uniforms worn by the Second Regiment during the Revolution were indigo blue.

Lowcountry - Area of South Carolina from the coast to about 50 miles inland. Today, it would be from the coast inland to approximately I-95. In Revolutionary War times rice and indigo were the major crops grown in the lowcountry.

Loyalists - Americans who decided to fight for the King of England - also called Tories.

Militia - Regular citizens who volunteered to fight battles and wars.

Parish - A unit of lands that today would be called a county in South Carolina.

Parole - Describes the action of captured soldiers from South Carolina who returned home and pledged not to take up arms against the King. Such was the case after the surrender of Charleston in 1780.

Partisans - Militia or citizen soldiers who fought a guerrilla war against the British Army.

Patriots - Citizens who fought for independence from England.

Plantation - A large farm - usually more than 100 acres in size.

Rampart - A fort's wall - often where cannons were mounted.

Rebels - The term used by the British to describe all citizens who fought against the British and Tory soldiers.

Regiment - A group of soldiers formed by the South Carolina Provincial Congress.

Regulars - Term used to describe professional soldiers who fought for Britain.

Tories - American citizens loyal to Britain - also called Loyalists.

Whigs - Americans who believed in and fought for independence from England.

Important Names to Remember

Lord **Cornwallis** - Commander of the British Army in the South

Colonel Welbore **Doyle** - British leader who tried to find Francis Marion

General Horatio **Gates** - Commander of Southern Continental Army - fled after being soundly beaten by the British at Camden

General Nathanael **Greene** - Replaced Gates as Commander of the Continental Army in South Carolina - worked closely with militia leaders

Peter **Horry** - Militia leader who fought alongside Francis Marion

Major John **James** - Williamsburg Militia leader who fought with Francis Marion

William **James** - Young son of Major James - also fought with Marion

Colonel Henry "Light Horse Harry" **Lee** - Calvary commander who fought alongside Francis Marion at the battles of Fort Watson and Fort Motte (father of RE Lee)

Hezekiah **Maham** - Militia soldier who designed "Maham's Tower", which helped the patriots defeat the British at Fort Watson

Francis **Marion** - "The Swamp Fox" - Native of South Carolina, who early in his military career fought in the Cherokee War-later used techniques of surprise and stealth to fight a guerrilla war against the British and Tory forces in the swamps of the Pee Dee region of South Carolina

General Daniel **Morgan** - Commander of all American forces at the Battle of Cowpens

Rebecca **Motte** - Owner of the plantation where Battle of Fort Motte took place

William **Moultrie** - Commander of South Carolina's 2nd Regiment at the battle of Fort Sullivan on June 28, 1776

Andrew **Pickens** - Militia leader in the northwestern part of South Carolina

Lord **Rawdon** - Commander of British forces in South Carolina in 1782 after Lord Cornwallis took his army to Virginia

John **Rutledge** - Governor of South Carolina during the Revolution - fled Charleston and continued to govern while running from the British

Thomas **Sumter** - "The Gamecock" - militia leader who fought in the middle of the state

Banastre **Tarleton** - Commanded the British Green Dragoon - mounted soldiers who wore green coats

General George **Washington** - Commander-In-Chief of the American Continental Army - also, first President of the United States of America

Major James **Weymss** - Brutal Tory leader

Bibliography

Bass, Robert D. Swamp Fox: The Life and Campaigns of General Francis Marion.
Sandlapper Publishing Co., Orangeburg, SC (2nd. Edition), 1974.

Bodie, Idella. The Revolutionary Swamp Fox.
Sandlapper Publishing Co., Orangeburg, SC, 1999.

Edgar, Walter. Partisans and Redcoats: The Southern Conflict that Turned the Tide of the American Revolution. HarperCollins Publishers, Inc., New York, NY, 2001.

Edgar, Walter. South Carolina: A History.
University of South Carolina Press, Columbia, SC, 1998.

Fraser, Walter J. Patriots, Pistols and Petticoats.
Charleston County Bicentennial Committee (Printed by RL Bryan Co. in Columbia), Charleston, SC, 1976.

Bibliography (cont.)

Gordon, John W. South Carolina and the American Revolution: A Battlefield History.
University of South Carolina Press, Columbia, SC, 2003.

Palmer, James and Sanford Adams. "Chasing the Swamp Fox", A Documentary film produced by SC ETV. (WWW.SCETV.ORG), Columbia, SC, 2005.

Wallace, David Duncan. South Carolina: A Short History.
University of South Carolina Press, Columbia, SC, 1966.

The Illustrator

James H. Palmer, Jr. grew up in Clemson, SC. He is a graduate of Clemson University. In January 2005, he wrote, illustrated, and co-produced "Chasing the Swamp Fox," a documentary about Francis Marion.

Fellow Clemson native and Clemson University graduate, Sanford Adams, a producer at South Carolina Educational Television, directed and co-produced the project.

James's meticulous research gave his computer artwork an authenticity that made Marion and his men come alive in moss-draped shadows and fiery battle.

Palmer, a graphic artist, lives in Atlanta, GA, with his wife Mandy and their son Leo.

The Author

Kate Salley Palmer is James Palmer's mother. A former nationally syndicated Editorial Cartoonist, she has written and illustrated several picture books for Warbranch Press, Inc., and has illustrated many more for other publishers. Her latest book, "Growing Up Cartoonist in the Baby Boom South," is a memoir and collection of her political cartoons.

Her first nonfiction book was "Palmetto: Symbol of Courage," the story of the famous Revolutionary War battle that produced a state tree for South Carolina, and led to the design of South Carolina's beauitful blue and white state flag.

Kate, originally from Orangeburg, South Carolina, lives now in Clemson with her husband, Jim, and their two dogs. Kate speaks about her books at schools, conferences and other groups.

South Carolina Revolutionary War Fighters

Native Americans

Fought in the Revolutionary War.

Cherokee
Fought on the British side.

Militia

Citizen soldiers who volunteered to fight with leaders such as Marion, Sumter, and Pickens

Catawba
Fought with the American partisans.

Tories
were citizen soldiers who fought for the British